EXPLORING HISTORY

NORTH AMERICA

BILL ASIKINACK AND KATE SCARBOROUGH

Belitha Press
In association with the Royal Geographical Society

Foreword

Many animals, birds and fish regularly travel over great distances. What sets people apart is the ability to explore and discover. An explorer is someone who is curious about the world and if you are curious enough to read this book then you too have become an explorer.

Exploring is not just about getting into a plane or sailing on a boat to a place you have never been to before – you have to record what you see, listen to the people you meet and learn about the place you find. This book follows in the footsteps of all good explorers by discovering the people, history and countryside of the land before it was discovered by outside peoples, as well as telling the stories of the adventurers who travelled there for the first time.

Explorers have travelled all over the world and have been helped throughout the centuries by the inhabitants of the lands they visited. People have shown outsiders their homes, helped them carry their loads, paddled their canoes, showed them amazing animals and often housed, clothed, fed, rescued and cured them. This book tells you about these people as well as the explorers they helped or fought with.

Travellers have explored the world for many different reasons. Early adventurers like Marco Polo (1254–1324) and Ibn Battuta (1304–1364) journeyed with trading caravans. Christopher Columbus (1451–1506), Ferdinand Magellan (1480–1521), Captain James Cook (1728–1779) and John Franklin (1786–1847) were sent by governments to investigate the geography of the world. Other explorers were merchants, scientists, colonialists, artists, adventurers, naturalists or even conquerors like Francisco Pizarro (1475–1541) who destroyed the Inca Empire he found.

The Royal Geographical Society is proud to support the *Exploration Into* series of books. Ever since it was founded in 1830, the RGS has helped and inspired famous explorers like Robert Scott (1868–1912) and Dr David Livingstone (1813–1873). Today, the RGS helps modern-day explorers climb the world's mountains, walk across its deserts, cycle through its continents, sail up its rivers, dive deep under the oceans and discover the scientific secrets of nature. We invite you to pick up *Exploration Into North America* and start your own journey of discovery…

DR JOHN HEMMING, *Director and Secretary, Royal Geographical Society, London*

The wide, open spaces and tall, scattered rocks of Monument Valley in Arizona. Native Americans such as the famous Apache and Navajo tribes lived and farmed in this region.

Contents

Buffalo Bull's Back Fat was chief of one of the Blackfoot nations. The Blackfoot lived in the north of the Great Plains.

1 Introduction

The Land

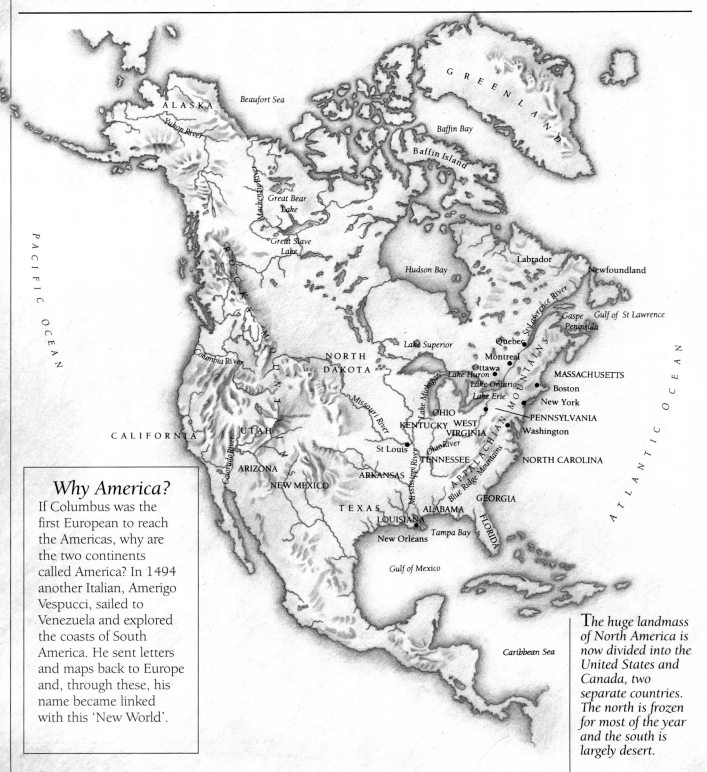

GREENLAND

ALASKA

Beaufort Sea

Yukon River

Mackenzie River

Baffin Bay

Baffin Island

Great Bear Lake

Great Slave Lake

Labrador

Hudson Bay

Newfoundland

PACIFIC OCEAN

ROCKY MOUNTAINS

Columbia River

St Lawrence River

Gaspe Peninsula

Gulf of St Lawrence

Quebec

Lake Superior

Montreal

Ottawa

NORTH DAKOTA

Lake Huron

MASSACHUSETTS

Lake Michigan

Lake Ontario

Boston

Lake Erie

New York

Missouri River

OHIO

PENNSYLVANIA

CALIFORNIA

UTAH

KENTUCKY

WEST VIRGINIA

Washington

St Louis

Ohio River

TENNESSEE

NORTH CAROLINA

ARIZONA

ARKANSAS

Colorado River

NEW MEXICO

Mississippi River

APPALACHIAN MOUNTAINS

Blue Ridge Mountains

TEXAS

ALABAMA

GEORGIA

LOUISIANA

New Orleans

Tampa Bay

FLORIDA

ATLANTIC OCEAN

Gulf of Mexico

Caribbean Sea

Why America?
If Columbus was the first European to reach the Americas, why are the two continents called America? In 1494 another Italian, Amerigo Vespucci, sailed to Venezuela and explored the coasts of South America. He sent letters and maps back to Europe and, through these, his name became linked with this 'New World'.

The huge landmass of North America is now divided into the United States and Canada, two separate countries. The north is frozen for most of the year and the south is largely desert.

The massive continent of North America stretches from the bitter north almost as far south as the **Equator**. The land has five major geographical regions. In the far north there is the cold **tundra**, a treeless and therefore shelterless area; in Canada the land is covered with forests and woods; the wide, flat plains of North America start near the Arctic and almost reach the Gulf of Mexico; finally there are two mountain ranges, the Rockies on the west coast and the Appalachians on the east.

The Climate

All these geographical areas have four seasons. In the north the winters are long and very cold while summers are short, and in the south the summers are hot and dry while winters rarely produce snow. Now imagine the kinds of people who lived in North America 500 years ago. Scattered over this vast and varied continent, they had very different ways of life depending on where they lived. They must have been very strong to survive in areas that might have been freezing cold or desperately hot and dry. In 1500 there were many different peoples in North America and more than 500 languages were spoken.

The Europeans

In 1492 Columbus sailed into the history books as the 'discoverer' of the Americas. At the time no one realized how dramatic the results of his landing would be. The events of the past 500 years tell the story of the effect colonization has had on the inhabitants of North America.

Exploring this Book

This book is divided into six chapters. The first one describes the migration of peoples to North America – the first explorers. The second looks at the different **nations** of the Native Americans. The next two chapters relate the exploration of North America by Europeans and the impact their arrival had on the Native Americans. Finally we look at North America today and the lives of modern-day Native Americans.

A huge totem pole made by the Native Americans of the north-west (see page 19). Totem poles stood outside the family's house; some of them were as tall as 15 metres.

Early Peoples

North America has many different climates. In Idaho spring flowers bloom in the valleys while there is snow on the mountain tops.

Arctic Ocean

SIBERIA

ALASKA

Ice Bridge

North Pacific Ocean

The Bering Strait as it might have been during the Ice Age when peoples moved from Siberia to Alaska. The outline shows where the ice may have covered the ocean.

People have inhabited North America for thousands of years. The idea that this continent was a 'New World' was thought up by those who arrived by ship from the other side of the Atlantic Ocean 500 years ago. The civilizations in North America were like those on the other side of the world. They had their own societies, customs, laws, religions, arts and rivalries. But where did they come from?

Migrating Peoples

The earliest human fossil remains found in North America are *Homo sapiens*, ancestors of ours who lived about 200,000 years ago. During an Ice Age about 50,000 years ago the ocean between Siberia and Alaska was probably bridged by a huge **glacier** which allowed people to migrate from one continent to the other.

A 19th-century engraving of an imaginary mammoth hunt. The people who migrated to North America were probably following the large animals they hunted for food.

The Mound Builders

Two groups of people formed the Adena and Hopewell cultures. They lived in the northern part of the Mississippi Valley. They probably arrived there from the south around 3500 BCE. They farmed the land and hunted, building their houses on circular mounds of earth. The Adenas and Hopewells also made burial mounds, some of which are still visible today. The most famous Adena mound is the serpent mound in Ohio. The Hopewell group were great traders; their goods have been found in areas ranging from the Gulf of Mexico up to the Great Lakes.

A *frog pipe made by a member of the Hopewell culture.*

As these original settlers travelled south through North America, they followed the herds of animals that were their prey. There were bison, mammoths, **mastodons,** giant sloths and beavers. These people (who are called Paleo-Indians by anthropologists) were big game hunters, particularly on the Great Plains and in the north-east. The enormous variety of arrowheads from this time show that they were very good at hunting. By 6000 BCE the **immigrants** had probably spread throughout the whole of North and South America.

From about 8000–1000 BCE people were settling down: they built villages and **domesticated** animals. Around the continent different peoples developed skills such as metal-working, art, trading and, by 1000 BCE, were farming in the east.

Why Indians?

Two and a half thousand years later when Columbus reached the Americas, he named the people he met 'los Indios' wrongly believing that the land he had found was India. This name became popular throughout Europe and has been used ever since, even though Indians have their own names. In this book when Indians are referred to as a group they are Native Americans.

T*he painting on these rocks in Arizona is ancient picture writing done by prehistoric Native Americans. This example is called the Newspaper Rock.*

2 Native American Cultures

People of the Far North

The far north of North America is often seen as a land of ice and snow. This is partly true, because the land is covered in snow for eight months of the year. The summers are short, but long enough for flowers to bloom and streams to run. The Inuit people live in this harsh environment, hunting seals and fishing in the freezing Arctic waters. Their way of life is totally adapted to life in the cold: they build houses from ice; travel on sledges pulled by hardy dogs and fish in boats (called umiaks and kayaks) made from animal bone and skin. The Inuit have always been strong believers in spirits that they think control and guide their lives. They pass down their beliefs from generation to generation through many stories and legends.

Lieutenant Hood, a British naval officer, painted this picture in 1820. It shows a Cree tent which has meat drying in the traditional way above a fire, as well as a more modern metal cooking pot.

Living in the Tundra

Just below the frozen Arctic is the vast tundra of northern Canada and central Alaska. The landscape is flat and almost treeless: most of the year temperatures are below freezing and very few plants grow. Although it may seem impossible, two separate groups of people live in this wasteland. The Athabaskans live to the west of central Alaska and in areas of northern Canada west of Hudson Bay. To the south and west of Hudson Bay are **Algonquian**-speaking people, who are linked to people living further south around the Great Lakes.

Hunting and Farming

The two groups survived in very different ways. The Athabaskans, whose major nations included the Chipewyan, Hare and Dogrib, hunted caribou, moose and bighorn sheep. They ate little vegetation because there was so little growing. The Algonquian-speaking nations, such as the Cree and Ojibwa (Chippewa), lived further south in more sheltered parts among the forests north of the Great Lakes. As well as hunting for deer, they also fished in the rivers with canoes they built from bark, like their cousins further south.

This photograph was taken in 1904 and shows a family of Alaskans. The father's name was Ethlota. These people lived much as the Athabaskans did, hunting for a living during the long winter and short summer.

Inuit Spirit World

The Inuit believe in a great number of spirits and demons. Some spirits are friendly, but most of them are hostile to humans. The Inuit therefore carve their spirits to look terrifying, as this model (left) shows. In order to keep themselves safe from these wicked spirits, the Inuit follow **rituals** which are conducted by shamans, medicine men. They make regular offerings to the spirits and say prayers over their dead and the animals that they hunt. For example, seals or whales that are killed are given a drink of water so that they can go to the spirit world saying that they were treated with respect. The shamans are also able to heal the sick.

The North-east

A Native American village camped on the edge of the Lake Huron, painted by Paul Kane in the 19th century. The nations in the north-east travelled the lakes in canoes.

This area extends from the Atlantic to and around the Great Lakes. The land is variable and so is the climate. There are stretches of rocky coastline, as well as **fertile** meadows, and rivers and streams spring from the Appalachian Mountains. The many nations in this area had much in common. They were hunters and farmers, as well as being excellent warriors.

The Iroquois

The **Iroquois** nations **evolved** around 1300 CE. They were the most able warriors of the region and often fought among themselves and against the Algonquian-speaking nations. Under the guidance of the famous Mohawk chief Hiawatha, five Iroquoian nations, the Onondaga, Mohawk, Seneca, Oneida and Cayuga, formed the League of Five Nations around 1560. This league encouraged peace among the Iroquois and created a united force against their enemies, such as the Huron nation. Shared problems and issues were discussed and dealt with by the Great Council, a group of 50 officials from each nation. What was unique about the League of Five Nations was that women held great power. They oversaw all the activities of the Great Council and chose those who were to enter the council, although the men made the final decisions.

Village Life

The Algonquian-speaking nations such as the Delawares in the south of this area relied on farming for their living. But the men of these nations were also hunters, fishermen, warriors and healers. The women were the farmers and the cooks. Their villages consisted of a central Big House, with their homes scattered around it. Each village also included a sweat house, which was used to cure all kinds of sickness.

All Algonquians relied on wild rice in their diets, and they also grew **tobacco** which was used during rituals and when socialising. These peoples had an all-powerful god called Manitou. During the summer months they held festivals in Manitou's honour.

The Iroquois were famous for their 'false face' society. Members of this group were asked to heal the sick, wearing masks like this one which were said to have healing powers.

An engraving of the Mohawk chief Hiawatha who founded the Iroquois League of Five Nations.

The South-east

The geographic area of the south-east reaches to the Mississippi River on the west, the Atlantic on the east, the present states of Tennessee and West Virginia in the north and the Gulf of Mexico in the south. The climate is mild, with plenty of rain to help plants grow. The rivers and coastline provide good fishing. The Native Americans who lived in this area became farmers, cultivating the lush land first with local plants such as sunflowers and **persimmon**. Later they grew **staple foods** such as potatoes, pumpkins, water melons, maize (corn) and tobacco.

Heavily Populated

This part of North America was the most densely populated by Native Americans: between 150 and 200 nations lived here. The main nations were the Iroquoian-speaking Cherokee, Chickasaw and Tuscarora in the north, the Powhatan and Chatawba on the coast, the Creek, Natchez and Choctaw towards the south and the Seminole in what is now called Florida.

Tobacco Smoking

Tobacco grew very well in the warm climate of the south-east. The habit of smoking tobacco became popular throughout North America and each nation had their own design of pipe, made from wood, stone or clay. The ritual of smoking pipes also developed, probably changing from a healing role to a peace-making one.

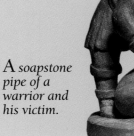

A soapstone pipe of a warrior and his victim.

The Mississippi River delta lies to the west of this region. Because of the river the land in the south-east is fertile and good for growing, but there are also swamp areas.

Five Civilized Tribes

The larger nations of this area were the Cherokee,
Chickasaw, Creek, Choctaw and Seminole who became
known by the European settlers as the Five Civilized
Tribes. This was because their societies were organized in
a way that was familiar to Europeans. For example, in the
Creek nations town councils met every day to discuss
problems and affairs. They had a very strong **clan** system,
which meant that families were loyal to each other. Creek
towns were set out around a public square, with summer
and winter council houses, a hot house for winter
activities and an open yard for games in summer. Their
houses were rectangular and built from wood with walls
plastered in mud and grass. There was always a hole in
the roof to allow smoke from the fire to escape. Each
house was occupied by several families of one clan.

Cherokee Villages

A Cherokee village surrounded a huge, seven-sided,
domed council house. It could hold up to 500 people
and was used during ceremonies and council meetings.
Around it were the games fields and farming land for the
whole community. On the edges of this land were the
Cherokees' small rectangular houses.

Native Americans throughout the east played team games. This one, painted by Charles Deas in 1843, is an early form of lacrosse.

A Cherokee chief called Stalking Turkey, painted in London by F. Parson in 1762.

The Great Plains

The Great Plains stretch from the Gulf of Mexico in the south to the tundra in the northernmost part of the continent. They start in the west at the Rocky Mountains and stop in the east at the Mississippi River. This is a land of blazing hot summers which reach temperatures of 38°C and bitterly cold winters with heavy snow in winter, when temperatures fall to −40°C.

The Wandering Life

The people who lived in this area were hunters and farmers. They grew corn, beans and **squash**, and hunted animals such as the enormous bison and birds. They travelled everywhere on foot (the Native American horse had died out in prehistoric times). There were many different nations in this vast region and they can be

Hunting the Bison

The horse in North America died out shortly after the last Ice Age, so the nations of the plains hunted bison on foot. In this painting by George Catlin (dating from 1832) two men covered in wolf skins attempt to frighten the bison towards another group of men (out of the picture) who lie in wait ready to spear the bison.

There is also evidence of another hunting method used by the Native Americans. They frightened and then chased a herd of bison over a cliff.

A group of Dakota men sit in their sweat lodge. Sitting in the sweat lodge cleansed their minds, bodies, hearts and spirits.

A late 19th-century photograph of an old Comanche man. Notice the beading and fur in his hair.

divided by their different ways of life. Some nations were **nomadic**, such as the Crow, Blackfoot, Arapahoe, Cheyenne and Comanche. They followed herds of bison around the plains. In the east there were semi-nomadic nations such as the Sioux, Omaha and Missouri who lived in permanent villages between the hunts. Each nation had its own identity with different clothing, houses and games. But they seemed to share the same religious beliefs.

Religious Festivals

At the beginning of summer every nation celebrated with the Sun Dance. People gave thanks to the sun and asked the guidance of the guardian spirit for the future. The ritual was led by a medicine person who said the prayers. The whole nation gathered for the Sun Dance and then they all set off for a joint hunt. This hunt was strictly organized: each member of the tribe had a different task. Scouts went ahead of the hunting party, while warriors defended them from the rear. The women packed up the belongings needed for the hunt on to a travois, a dog-drawn sledge.

When Europeans arrived in the 15th century they brought horses with them. This eventually changed the way of life on the Great Plains. Riding horses, the Native Americans in this area were able to travel greater distances much faster and hunting became far easier.

The South-west

The remains of the beautiful city of Mesa Verde in Arizona built into the rock face (right). The Zuni people were the architects.

The modern states of Arizona and New Mexico make up the south-west of North America. Two separate groups of Native Americans lived here, farmers such as the Zuni and Hopi nations (nicknamed Pueblos, which means town in Spanish) and hunter-gatherers such as the Navajo and Apache nations.

Anasazi

The Anasazi people started farming in the south-west more than 2,500 years ago. Because the area was very dry, they built irrigation systems that had developed into huge networks of canals by AD 600. With the water they were able to cultivate corn, cotton and beans. By AD 700 they were building stone dwellings which developed into cities. Their artistic skills are also seen on the black and white pottery they made. They did hunt using spears (like these on the right), but this was less important than farming to them.

Builders and artists

The Zuni and Hopi nations are well-known for their architectural and artistic skills. They built large cities out of the red sandstone in the area. One city, called Pueblo Bonito (meaning beautiful town), used a system of heating similar to one used today to conserve energy. This is called **passive solar heating** and relies on the heat from the sun to warm rooms. The 'pueblo' artistic skills can be seen clearly in the way the people dressed and decorated themselves.

The women wore cloth dresses tied on the right shoulder. Young women wore their hair in an elaborate squash-blossom style which could take over an hour to create. After they married they just plaited their hair. They made jewellery from turquoise and wore beaded necklaces.

The Hopi and Zuni nations farmed squash, corn, beans and tobacco. They also domesticated the turkey, which was introduced to Europe by Spanish explorers and has become very popular since, especially at Christmas.

Navajo and Apache Nations

The Navajo nation were originally nomads and settled in the area in the 15th century. They learnt to build houses called hogans, but they did not build cities, preferring to live in smaller groups. They farmed the land and raised sheep. The Apaches were the other nation to come from the north. Like the Navajo they spoke Athabaskan. They continued to be nomadic and spread themselves throughout the south-west area. They were a fearsome nation skilled in warfare and produced many great Native American leaders, such as Geronimo (see page 41).

A Navajo blanket woven with a corn plant in the middle and two sacred figures on either side. Around them is a rainbow. This blanket was probably made in the 19th century.

*The Hopi spirits that were involved with the yearly cycle of birth, death and rebirth were called **katchinas**. This doll represents a katchina spirit and was made from cotton wood and decorated with feathers and paint.*

The Great Basin and the North-west

The Great Basin is divided into two regions: the southern part is a harsh desert, while the north is more **habitable** because of the rivers running through it. The Indians in the south, the Shosone, Ute and Bannock had difficult lives, and spent all their time surviving. They were nomadic and travelled around in search of food, which included plants, insects (especially locusts), and the few animals that lived in this region. In the north of the basin the people developed a rich culture because survival there was easier. There was plenty of game, as well as fish, wild nuts and berries. They mixed with other Native Americans from the subarctic, the north-west and the plains and traded successfully with them. When they came across Europeans, they welcomed them and generally allowed trappers and hunters to share in the fruits of the area.

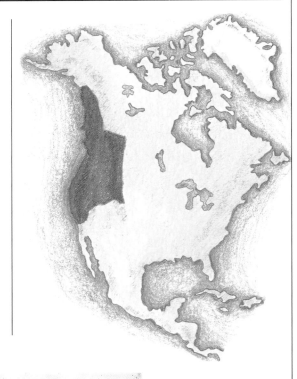

The dry landscape of the red canyon in Utah where the people of the Great Basin scratched out a living.

A Bannock family camped near Medicine Lodge Creek in Idaho. This photograph was taken in 1871. These people were nomads.

The cold landscape of the north-west, with the mountain of Stek-ya-den in the background.

A robe worn by a high ranking man at a potlatch ceremony.

Totem People

On the north-west coast between the Rockies and the Pacific Ocean the land is also fertile. Here there are plenty of wild fruits and also a wide variety of animals. The people of this area, such as the Tlingit, Haida, Kwakiutl and Chinook, developed skills beyond hunting and farming. They built log houses from massive cedar planks and travelled through the rivers in elaborately carved 20-metre-long dugout boats.

Their carving was most strikingly shown off on the huge totem poles which were displayed next to every house in the village. Early **missionaries** to the area were terrified by these poles, thinking that they were gifts to the **pagan gods**. But they had nothing to do with religion. They were more like the coats of arms displayed by some families in Europe. Each family's totem pole told stories about particular animals or spirits that were passed down from generation to generation.

The totem pole is only one example of the art of the north-west cultures, but there would have been a lot more. Other cedar carvings would have rotted over the years. The totem poles have survived because they were exposed to sunlight in the open air.

A cedar wood mask made by the Bella Coola nation.

Potlatch

The Native Americans of the north-west developed a ceremony called potlatch to share their wealth. A rich man would hold an enormous party, inviting hundreds of guests. They would arrive in their best boats, wearing their best clothes, ready for up to ten days of feasting. There would be singing and dancing and the host and his clan were toasted. To show how wealthy he was, the host would send his guests away with all his possessions. Some potlatch hosts are reported to have given away thousands of elaborately woven blankets. This party could bankrupt the host, but he could rely on being invited to his neighbour's potlatch and there receive a pile of gifts himself.

When Europeans arrived in the region they misunderstood the ceremony, thinking again that it had something to do with pagan practices. Missionaries insisted that the government ban the event.

19

3 The Savage Invasion

The First Explorers

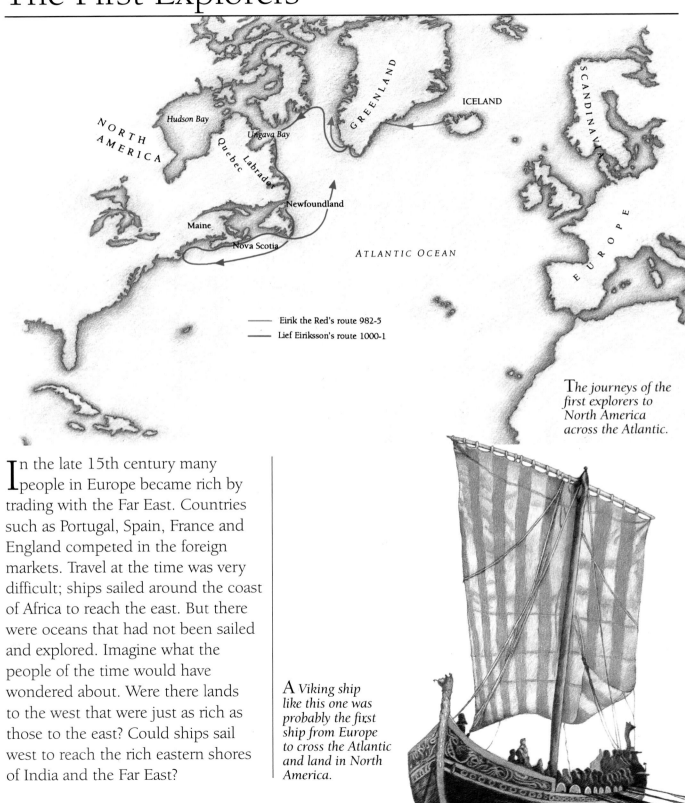

NORTH AMERICA

Hudson Bay

Ungava Bay

Quebec

Labrador

Newfoundland

Maine

Nova Scotia

GREENLAND

ICELAND

SCANDINAVIA

EUROPE

ATLANTIC OCEAN

——— Eirik the Red's route 982-5
——— Lief Eiriksson's route 1000-1

The journeys of the first explorers to North America across the Atlantic.

In the late 15th century many people in Europe became rich by trading with the Far East. Countries such as Portugal, Spain, France and England competed in the foreign markets. Travel at the time was very difficult; ships sailed around the coast of Africa to reach the east. But there were oceans that had not been sailed and explored. Imagine what the people of the time would have wondered about. Were there lands to the west that were just as rich as those to the east? Could ships sail west to reach the rich eastern shores of India and the Far East?

A Viking ship like this one was probably the first ship from Europe to cross the Atlantic and land in North America.

The Vikings

Everyone thinks that Christopher Columbus was the first to sail the Atlantic and discover the Americas in 1492. This is not strictly true. Almost 500 years earlier Vikings from Scandinavia reached the eastern coast of what they called Vinland. There is evidence that the Vikings built settlements on Newfoundland, Labrador and Ungava Bay (Northern Quebec).

Stories tell of Leif Eiriksson, the son of a Viking called Eirik the Red, sailing from Greenland. The settlements he set up soon disappeared, but they prove that Columbus was not the first to reach the Americas.

Fishermen from Europe

There are also stories told by the Micmac people, who fish around Newfoundland, that fishermen (whom they called hairy faces) from France and Portugal fished off the coast and landed to clean their catch. These stories date from the middle of the 15th century, again before Columbus.

Exploration to the west began in earnest in the late 15th century with Columbus' epic journey in 1492. He was followed by explorers from France, the Netherlands, England and Russia. There were many different reasons why these people wanted to make such difficult journeys: the lure of gold, adventure, a new life, trade, land. Whatever the reason, they were to have a dramatic effect on life in North and South America.

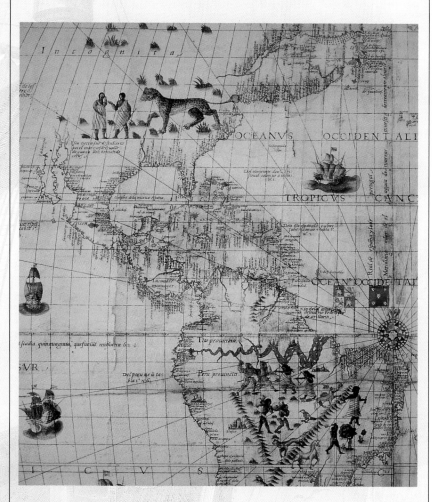

John Cabot

The Italian explorer John Cabot (his real name was Giovanni Cabotti) was sent by the English King Henry VII in 1497 to find a new way to the East Indies. Cabot sailed west, following in the path of Columbus, but started off much further north. He landed somewhere on the coast of Maine or Nova Scotia, convinced that he had reached the east. He explored the north-east coast and returned to England with news of land found and excellent fishing grounds. Henry was encouraged by these results and sent Cabot off again the next year, but on the return trip his ship went down.

The English lost interest in these discoveries as they did not bring the promised wealth of the east. It was not for another 50 years that England renewed its exploration of North America. The map above of the east coast of North America was drawn up in 1544 by Cabot's son, Sebastian.

The Spanish Search for Gold

The first land that Columbus and his men saw was a small island in the Bahamas. They sailed on to Cuba and then Hispaniola (modern-day Haiti). They were given a little gold by the islanders, which impressed the king and queen of Spain when they returned. Over the next 20 years, the Spanish established **colonies** on the islands and explored Central and South America. They discovered many different peoples and were greatly impressed by the wealth they found.

Sighting Florida

In 1513 a 53-year-old Spaniard called Juan Ponce de León sighted and landed on the **peninsula** of Florida. He was looking for a mythical island where a magic mountain was said to make old men young again. More important were the stories that people were telling about very wealthy

This picture of Columbus meeting Native Americans in 1492 was painted nearly 100 years later by the Spanish illustrator de Bry in 1590.

The map shows the journeys of de León, Narváez, de Soto and Coronado. They came from Central America and explored the lands of the south-east.

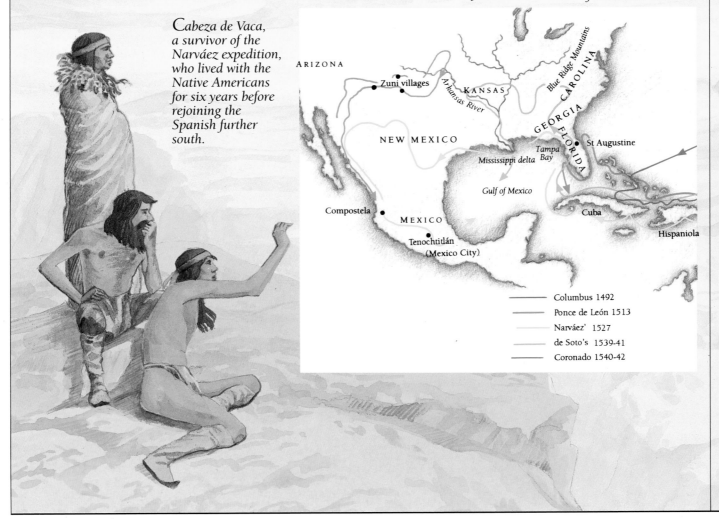

Cabeza de Vaca, a survivor of the Narváez expedition, who lived with the Native Americans for six years before rejoining the Spanish further south.

ARIZONA

Zuni villages

KANSAS

Arkansas River

Blue Ridge Mountains

CAROLINA

GEORGIA

FLORIDA

St Augustine

NEW MEXICO

Tampa Bay

Mississippi delta

Gulf of Mexico

Cuba

Compostela

MEXICO

Hispaniola

Tenochtitlán
(Mexico City)

———— Columbus 1492
———— Ponce de León 1513
———— Narváez' 1527
———— de Soto's 1539-41
———— Coronado 1540-42

civilizations living on the mainland. These stories seemed to come true when the Aztec civilization was found in Mexico. This inspired other adventurers to explore the North American mainland to see what they could find.

In Search of Gold

One such adventurer was the **conquistador** Pánfilo de Narváez who sailed from Spain in 1527 to search for the Seven Cities of Cibola, cities said to be even richer than the Aztec home of Tenochtitlán. With 300 men and 42 horses he marched north from Tampa Bay through glades and marshland. The expedition ended in disaster with Narváez missing and others captured by the people who lived in the region.

Survivors of this expedition found their way back to Spanish settlements and told others that there may still be rich nations further north. This started two other great expeditions into the interior. Hernando de Soto launched a journey into the south-east in 1539, and Francisco Vásquez de Coronado set out in 1540 in the south-west.

Hernando de Soto

Hernando de Soto reached Tampa Bay in May 1539. The Native Americans signalled to one another warning of the presence of white men. These warnings were needed. De Soto was very cruel to the people he met, hunting them as slaves, throwing them to hungry dogs and killing them if they tried to escape.

In spite of his cruelty, de Soto found no gold in Florida, none in Georgia, the Blue Ridge Mountains of North Carolina or South Carolina.

In May 1541 he found the Mississippi River and crossed it. He would not give up and died on the expedition. Under the command of Luis de Moscoso, the remaining soldiers built boats and sailed down the Mississippi to the safety of the Gulf of Mexico.

Francisco Vásquez de Coronado

The second expedition inspired by the stories of survivors such as Cabeza de Vaca was led by Francisco Vásquez de Coronado. He travelled with 270 soldiers and nearly 1,000 Native Americans. They marched into what is now Arizona and on to New Mexico. Here they met various Zuni nations in their great cities, but no gold. Again the Spanish force and the Native Americans clashed, for Coronado was as cruel as de Soto had been. But in 1542 Coronado returned to Mexico a ruined man.

Hernando de Soto used the Native Americans he found as slaves on his expedition, as did the other Spanish explorers. They were very cruel to the people and had no respect for the civilizations they came across and often destroyed.

Early Settlers

The Spanish were not the only people who colonized North America in the 16th century. Further along the east coast the French and English were laying claim to land in the names of their rulers.

West to China?

In 1534 King Francis of France granted Jacques Cartier permission to try and find a short cut to China by heading west across the Atlantic. Cartier had plenty of experience in Atlantic waters: he had fished in the North Atlantic and spent several years attacking Spanish ships. Cartier reached Newfoundland 20 days after leaving France. He continued north into the Gulf of St Lawrence, finally anchoring just south of the Gaspe peninsula, which he claimed and called New France. Here he met Micmac people who welcomed the sailors and were more than willing to trade.

Returning to France, Cartier took with him two of the Huron chief's sons, Domagaia and Taignagny. In 1535 Cartier returned to North America with the Huron men, who must have told him of the great river that flows west. He called it the Hochelaga River, which was its Huron name (but it later became the St Lawrence River). The ship put in at the Huron village of Stadacona, where the chief Donnacona was said to be ruler of Canada – hence the name for this land. Sailing further upstream he reached the village of Hochelaga.

Again he was met by friendly people, who told him that further up the river there were rapids which meant that he could go no further. This was no route through to China.

In 1541 Cartier tried to establish a French colony in North America, but his attempt failed. The good relationship that Cartier had with the Native Americans allowed a busy fur trade to develop.

Cartier's journey into New France and the settlements of the English on the east coast.

John White was the governor of the settlement on the island of Roanoke and he was also a painter. He recorded many scenes from the lives of the Native Americans around him. Here he shows the Native Americans using spears and nets to catch fish.

A *French map drawn up in 1546 of the lands in North America (now Canada) explored by Jacques Cartier in 1542.*

Sir Walter Raleigh

Early English Settlers

The English finally decided to enter the 'New World' in the late 16th century as a result of their rivalry with the Spanish. They thought that a North American settlement would be a good base from which they could attack Spanish territories. Two men were particularly keen for this to happen: Humphrey Gilbert and Walter Raleigh. Gilbert's attempt to form a settlement in 1578 failed, but he claimed Newfoundland in 1583 for Queen Elizabeth I. Raleigh did not do much better: his colony on the island of Roanoke in 1587 ended in the disappearance of all 116 settlers.

The dream of an English settlement did not die. In 1606 Captain John Smith and 150 colonists established themselves in a place they called Jamestown, Virginia. At first things did not go well. John Smith was persuaded to approach the Powhatan nation for help. The Powhatans decided to kill him, but Smith was lucky. Pocahontas, the chief's daughter, saved him from death and for the next 16 years there was peace between the settlers and the Powhatans.

Pocahontas

Pocahontas, daughter of the Powhatan chief, saved John Smith's life when she was only 12. It seems surprising that a girl could have such power, but the Powhatans considered women very important. In 1614 she married another settler, John Rolfe. He took her back to England where she became known as Lady Rebecca. She learned the English language and customs. While she was in England she also had a child. Sadly, at only 21 she died in London from smallpox.

Mapping the Interior

While the English were settling in Jamestown, the French decided to strengthen their hold on the north-east by encouraging fur traders to settle there. This was not entirely successful. The French geographer Samuel de Champlain explored further inland and claimed what he found for France. In 1603 he sailed up the St Lawrence River to Hochelaga. While he **charted** the area, some local people told him of a massive waterfall to the west – the Niagara Falls. On several other expeditions over the next few years, Champlain mapped the coast down to Maine, Massachusetts Bay and what was to become Plymouth Harbour (when the Pilgrim Fathers arrived in 1620). In 1608 Champlain led a small expedition up the St Lawrence River to a place not far from the old Huron village of Stadacona. This became a trading post called Quebec.

Champlain still believed that the St Lawrence River might be the route to the east and determined to find out.

Learning Algonquian

In 1610 Champlain returned to France leaving behind a young Frenchman, Etienne Brulé, with the Algonquian. When Champlain returned Brulé was able to translate the Algonquian reports, which helped the French to explore. But Champlain gave up his quest to reach China after a hazardous journey up the Ottawa River. He did manage to push through to Georgian Bay and Lake Ontario, but was forced back by Iroquois. This route was used by French traders for years to come.

The Pilgrim Fathers

While the French were exploring the Great Lakes, the Pilgrim Fathers crept into Plymouth Harbour in November 1620. The ship, the *Mayflower*, had been sailing for two months carrying 102 people to their new life. When they landed in what was to be called New England they had to prepare themselves for winter, but they were

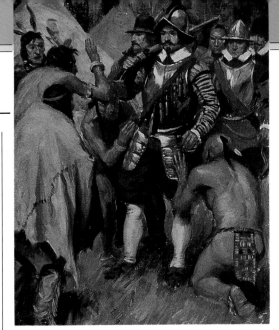

Samuel de Champlain's first meeting with the Hurons of the north-east.

Champlain and the Iroquois

On Champlain's first journey up the St Lawrence River, he was befriended by the Huron and Algonquian nations. Their great enemies were the Iroquois nations, with whom they had constant battles for territory. Champlain took part in one of these battles, killing three Iroquois chiefs. The French were to pay dearly for their alliance with the Huron and Algonquian nations.

George Henry Boughton's late 19th-century painting of the landing of the Pilgrim Fathers. The soldiers listen to readings from the Bible.

A late 19th-century painting by J.L. Ferris of the Pilgrim Fathers celebrating their first harvest with the Native Americans who had taught them how to survive.

not hunters and could not plant in frozen ground. They survived, thanks to the help of the local people. In March 1621 a tall Native American walked into the Pilgrims' settlement and said 'Welcome Englishmen'. This man was Samoset, chief of the Pemaquid people. He had learnt English from fishermen. Shortly after Samoset's visit, two other Native Americans, Massasoit, chief of the Wampanoags, and Squanto welcomed the settlers. Squanto had been captured by earlier English explorers and taken to England, where he had lived for several years. He taught the settlers where to fish, how to plant corn and how to hunt. The following autumn the pilgrims celebrated their harvest with the Native Americans. This was the first Thanksgiving.

French Adventurers

In the early 17th century a new type of French adventurer arose in New France. Young men, who wanted to explore further inland and succeed in fur trading, adopted a life similar to the Native Americans. They were able to look after themselves alone in the forests. The name they gave themselves, *coureur de bois,* means forest runner.

One such man, Jean Nicolet, was **commissioned** by Champlain in 1634 to travel further up the Great Lakes to see whether there was a way through to the east. His journey took him to Green Bay on Lake Michigan, where instead of finding oriental people he was greeted by the Winnebago people. They were greatly impressed by the Chinese robes he was wearing and treated him royally. But Champlain never heard the results of this voyage. He died on Christmas Day, 1635.

An illustration by Frederic Remington of a coureur de bois *trading with a Native American.*

Down the Mississippi

While the French and the English were establishing their new lands, in 1625 the Dutch landed on Manhattan island, calling it New Amsterdam. They bought the island from the Native Americans for about £15.

New Amsterdam (now known as New York) in 1650.

Relations with the Native Americans at this time were not always peaceful. In New England the Puritans were expanding rapidly. The Native Americans were being driven from their hunting and farming lands. They tried to defend their territory, but in 1637 the settlers massacred a whole Pequot village. Again in 1643 the Dutch in New Amsterdam were having problems settling into the lands of the Wappinger nation, whose livelihood depended on being able to hunt and fish in their territory. The Dutch solution was to slaughter hundreds of Native Americans.

Establishing New France

The French attempt to settle in New France seemed to stand still until the late 17th century. In 1660 there were only 3,000 permanent residents, compared with almost a million English colonists on the east coast. The area was difficult to settle because farming the land was a struggle, the Iroquois nation were hostile to the French and trade was drying up. Louis XIV, the French Sun King, stepped in to save his new lands. He sent a military force and appointed a colonial **governor.**

To the Great River

Once the colony started to thrive, the French turned to exploration. Two men, Médart Chouart des Groseilliers and Pierre Ésprit Radisson, had ventured further west than anyone through the Great Lakes. But there were rumours of a great river that ran south from the lakes.

Metacom, chief of the Wampanoags

In 1620 the Pilgrim Fathers made peace with the Wampanoags through their chief Massasoit. This peace lasted until his death in 1662. In 1675 as the settlements in Massachusetts were spreading, Massasoit's son Metacom (known to the settlers as King Philip) led a group of nations against the settlers. For three years the local nations fought against the Europeans only to lose. By 1700 the Wampanoag nation had almost disappeared.

Louis Joliet and Father Marquette exploring the Mississippi with friendly Native Americans in 1673.

La Salle's expedition reached the mouth of the Mississippi where a cross was set up in 1682. La Salle claimed the whole of the Mississippi Valley for France. This painting is by George Catlin, who was a famous American painter of Native Americans and their history.

The first person commissioned to find it was Louis Joliet. In 1673 he and a priest called Father Jacques Marquette travelled to Green Bay and on to the Fox River. From there they carried their canoes to the Wisconsin River, which they followed to where it met the Mississippi. They heard from the locals that there were Spaniards further south and decided to turn back so that they could be sure to pass on their charts and records.

Robert Cavalier, Sieur de la Salle

The man who took up the challenge of the Mississippi was Robert Cavalier, Sieur de la Salle. In 1679 La Salle with his close friend Henri de Tonti set out from the Niagara River in the *Griffin*. They covered more than 150 kilometres a day, sailing into Lake Erie, Lake Huron and Lake Michigan. Along the way they stopped to trade with Native Americans and when the *Griffin* was heavy with furs La Salle sent it back to Lake Erie. For the next two years La Salle established trading posts and forts in the west. It was not until 1682 that La Salle finally sailed all the way down the Mississippi to the Gulf of Mexico. He claimed the whole of the Mississippi Valley for France, calling it Louisiana, after the French king, Louis XIV.

Hudson Bay

Labrador

Newfoundland

Gulf of St Lawrence

Gaspe Peninsula

Lake Superior

Quebec Maine

Nova Scotia

Ottawa River

Georgian Bay Montreal

Green Bay

St Lawrence River

Lake Champlain

Bay of Fundy

Lake Huron

Massachusetts Bay

Plymouth Harbour

Cape Cod

Lake Ontario

Niagara Falls

Lake Erie

Illinois River

Lake Michigan

NORTH ATLANTIC OCEAN

Arkansas River

Mississippi River

— Champlain's route 1603-15
— Brulé's route 1610-20
— Nicolet's route 1634
— Groseilliers' route 1654-57
--- Groseilliers' and Radisson's route 1659-63
— Joliet's and Marquette's route 1673
— La Salle's route 1679-82

This map shows the routes the French explorers and traders followed in the 1600s as they travelled westwards.

4 Colonization

European Rivalries

As the settlements expanded, rivalries between them grew. These were encouraged by the battles back home. The English were especially aggressive in gaining land. In 1664 the Duke of York claimed New Netherlands. He sent a fleet of warships to capture New Amsterdam. The Dutch governor, Peter Stuyvesant, had no choice but to give in. This sparked a war in Europe in 1667 between England and the Netherlands which resulted in defeat for the Netherlands. In the **Treaty** of Breda, signed at the end of the war, the Netherlands had to give up all its lands in North America. And in 1670 after war with Spain, the Treaty of Madrid forced the Spanish to acknowledge England's rights to lands in North America.

England's colonies were growing fast at this time and becoming much more established. In 1681 the **Quaker** leader William Penn was granted land in return for money that King Charles II owed his father. This land was called Pennsylvania. Penn was very keen to make peace with the local nations and for 75 years there was **stability** between the colonizers and the locals.

Peter Stuyvesant, the Dutch governor of New Amsterdam.

The division of lands in North America around 1700.

Chief Tishcohan was one of the chiefs with whom William Penn signed a treaty in 1681 as he formed the colony of Pennsylvania.

RUPERTS LAND

NEW FRANCE

NEWFOUNDLAND

NOVA SCOTIA

APPALACHIAN MOUNTAINS

LOUISIANA

THIRTEEN COLONIES

VICE-ROYALTY OF NEW SPAIN

FLORIDA

British possessions in 1700

French possessions in 1700

Spanish possessions in 1700

Areas claimed by British and French

More Fighting

The end of the 17th century and the beginning of the 18th century in North America saw war between the colonizers. Between 1689 and 1697 a series of battles (which became known as King William's War) between France allied with the Huron and Algonquian nations, and the English allied with the Iroquois, were fought for control of New York, New England and the Hudson Bay. From 1701 to 1713 the French and the Spanish fought the English in Queen Anne's War over rights to New England, Florida and South Carolina. The English won, adding Newfoundland and Acadia (now Nova Scotia) to their territories.

Georgia and Ohio

In 1733 James Oglethorpe set up a colony in North America for the poor of England to start a new life. This place became Georgia. Again the settlers were given land and although the Native Americans of the area, such as the Creeks, were consulted, they had little choice about giving over their lands.

In 1740 the next major war between the colonizers broke out. King George's War led to the English capturing the French fort of Louisbourg. It was a short-lived victory because the peace agreement in 1748 made the English hand the fort back. The following year the English king granted 80,000 hectares of land in the Ohio valley to a people from Virginia. This region had been claimed by the French who were building forts to secure their ownership. In 1754 Fort Duquesne was built (on the land that is now Pittsburgh) and the next year the Virginians sent a force under General Braddock to attack it. The attack was a disaster and the general and many men were killed.

William Penn used trade and diplomacy to agree a treaty with the Native Americans which kept peace between the settlers and the locals for 75 years. You can see the signatures on the contract Penn is holding.

The Defeat of France

An engraving of the siege and capture of the city of Quebec from the French by the British under the command of General Wolfe in 1759.

The defeat of the Virginian force at Fort Duquesne spurred the English to further their attacks on French property. In 1756 the Seven Years' War started in Europe. In North America this was seen as a continuation of the struggle for the Ohio Valley.

The French seemed to be stronger as they had successfully fought off the British. But the efforts of three British men changed the course of American history: George Washington, Sir William Johnson and William Pitt.

George Washington was responsible for training the army. He realized that an alliance with the Native Americans was vital. Washington knew that 'Indians are the only match for Indians, and without these we shall ever fight upon unequal terms'.

Sir William Johnson held together the British alliance with the Iroquois which was beginning to fail. He lived among the Mohawk and was equally at home with the British and Native Americans. He married the sister of the great Mohawk chief Joseph Brant and looked after the interests of the Mohawks.

A portrait by George Romney of the Chief of the Mohawks, Joseph Brant, who was a close friend of William Johnson and an ally of the British.

William Pitt planned a strategy for victory 3,000 miles away from North America. By 1758 the plan had succeeded and the British had taken Fort Duquesne, Louisbourg and Fort Frontenac. These cut off French links from St Lawrence to Ohio.

The Capture of Quebec

The most important British victory during this time was the capture of Quebec. In 1759 a young general, James Wolfe, marched to Quebec where the Marquis de Montcalm was preparing to defend the city. The city had been besieged for two months when some British ships managed to slip through the French defences. This allowed the British to scale the walls. A battle followed and both Montcalm and Wolfe were killed. The city surrendered. Shortly after Montreal also fell into British hands.

In 1763 the French were defeated and the Treaty of Paris divided the lands of North America between the British and the Spanish.

The Royal Proclamation

In the same year as the Treaty of Paris was signed so too was a treaty with the Native Americans, the royal proclamation. The British drew a line along the Appalachian Mountains, stating that no settlements should be allowed west of it. This was to be Native American territory. This did not satisfy some of the Native Americans who had lost faith in the British. Pontiac, chief of the Ottawa nation, led the attack on various frontier settlements. The Ottawas were defeated. They were not able to prevent British settlers from moving west as indeed they did, in spite of the royal proclamation.

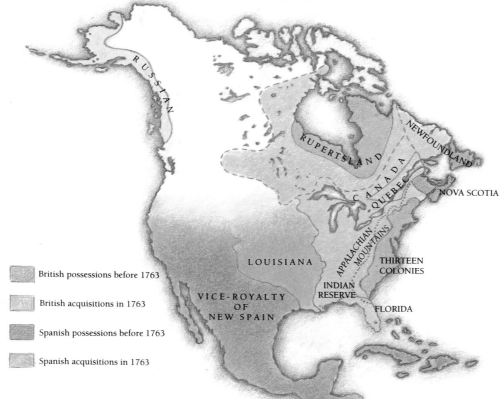

British possessions before 1763

British acquisitions in 1763

Spanish possessions before 1763

Spanish acquisitions in 1763

RUSSIAN

RUPERTSLAND

NEWFOUNDLAND

CANADA

QUEBEC

NOVA SCOTIA

LOUISIANA

APPALACHIAN MOUNTAINS

THIRTEEN COLONIES

INDIAN RESERVE

VICE-ROYALTY OF NEW SPAIN

FLORIDA

Compare this map of the new territorial claims in 1763 with the claims in 1700 on page 30. The British and Spanish have shared out all the French territory. The Spanish took French lands in central North America, because they had helped the French during the war. But they had to give up Florida to the British.

33

Independence

The men and women who decided to ignore the royal proclamation moved west, no longer fearing attack from the French. They did have to face the Native Americans who were trying to protect their lands. One man in particular, Daniel Boone, led the way west. He was born in the state of Pennsylvania and spent his youth learning how to survive in the wild. In 1769 Boone set out with a few friends from North Carolina, heading towards Kentucky. They followed the Native Americans' Warrior's Path through the forests and over the mountains into Kentucky. This time they were exploring, but in 1775 Boone led a group of pioneer settlers who set up homes in this very fertile land.

The Fight for Land

As the colonizers moved west, they seemed to forget that the land belonged to others. The Native Americans often welcomed the settlers, but as soon as the settlers were able to look after themselves, they drove the Native Americans away. Some nations moved away quietly, others stood their ground. The main difference between these people was that the Native Americans always saw the land as belonging to the community to be worked for the good of all. They did not understand or believe in the idea that one person should own a piece of land.

Daniel Boone led settlers through the Appalachian Mountains to the west in the late 18th century. George Celeb Bingham painted this picture 50 years later.

George Washington

Colonization

The War of Independence was sparked off by fighting in Boston. The settlers were furious at the amount of tax they had to pay the British government on goods such as tea. When the next cargo of tea arrived in the Boston harbour, they threw it into the sea. Soldiers were sent into the town and the result was a massacre of the protesting settlers.

Smallpox

When the first settlers arrived in North America, they brought with them diseases common in Europe. These diseases were new to North America, and the Native Americans suffered terribly from them. Smallpox was one of the biggest killers of the Native Americans. In 1712 the North Carolina nations suffered its effects and in 1738 half the Cherokee nation was wiped out by smallpox. Reports from fur traders told of the horror this disease brought: 'None of us had the least idea of the desolation this dreadful disease had done, until we went up the bank to the camp and looked into the tents in many of which they were all dead.'

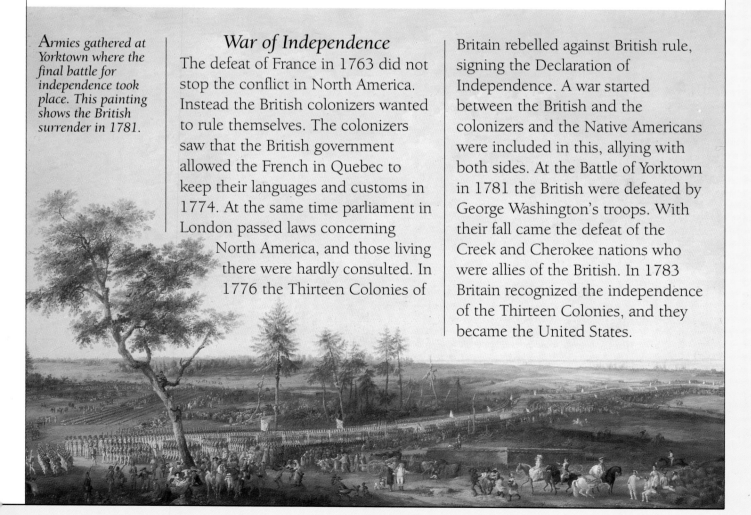

Armies gathered at Yorktown where the final battle for independence took place. This painting shows the British surrender in 1781.

War of Independence

The defeat of France in 1763 did not stop the conflict in North America. Instead the British colonizers wanted to rule themselves. The colonizers saw that the British government allowed the French in Quebec to keep their languages and customs in 1774. At the same time parliament in London passed laws concerning North America, and those living there were hardly consulted. In 1776 the Thirteen Colonies of Britain rebelled against British rule, signing the Declaration of Independence. A war started between the British and the colonizers and the Native Americans were included in this, allying with both sides. At the Battle of Yorktown in 1781 the British were defeated by George Washington's troops. With their fall came the defeat of the Creek and Cherokee nations who were allies of the British. In 1783 Britain recognized the independence of the Thirteen Colonies, and they became the United States.

35

5 The Fight for Land

Further West

The royal proclamation of 1763 did not stop colonizers moving further west, nor did it prevent them from trying to take over the lands of the Native Americans. The Native Americans had been divided during . the War of Independence, but both sides suffered losses. Those who had been on the losing British side faced hostility from the now superior forces of the United States. The Cherokee nation had been on the losing side and in 1785 had to accept a treaty with the United States government. They handed over all their land east of the Blue Ridge.

Lewis and Clark reached the Columbia River on their way across North America. The map below shows the route they took from 1804 to 1806.

Lewis and Clark

The transcontinental journey of Lewis and Clark in 1804–6 opened the way to new lands in the far west.

Meriwether Lewis and William Clark were sent by Thomas Jefferson, the President of the United States at the time, to find the source of the Missouri River and from there to travel to the Pacific coast. Lewis and Clark took with them several Native Americans, whom they used as interpreters on the way. One of the interpreters was a Shosone woman, called Sacagawea, who was pregnant at the time and had her baby on the journey.

Lewis and Clark were among the first white people to meet the nations of the north-west, such as the Chinook, Tlingit and Haida. These people were friendly towards the explorers, and did not feel threatened by settlers, unlike the nations in the east and on the plains.

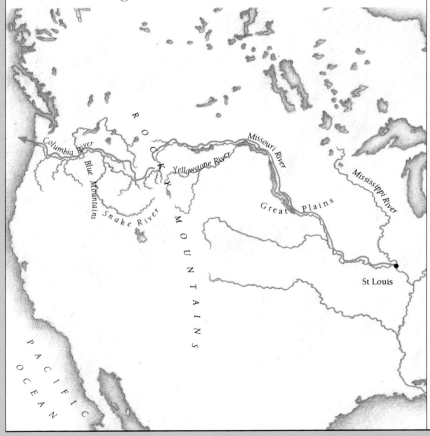

Late Resistance

There were still nations in the east and on the plains who were prepared to fight for their land. Around the late 1700s Alex McGillivray, the half-Creek, half-Scot leader of the Creeks, unified his people against the settlements. Later the Shawnee chief Tecumseh gathered support among the nations on the east coast. Tecumseh's force faced the settlers at Tippecanoe River in 1811, but they were defeated.

Border Disputes

The British and the United States were at war again in 1812, fighting over the border between the States and Canada. The Native Americans saw the British as allies in their struggle to keep their lands and many of them joined the war. Tecumseh was one of these and he was killed as he tried to reach the safety of Canada. With the British defeat, the Native Americans were again on the losing side. They were continually harassed by the settlers. A United States general and statesman Andrew Jackson attacked the Creeks in the south-east, forcing them to give up their lands in Georgia and Alabama. In 1830 the states of Mississippi, Alabama and Georgia banned Native American settlements. Then in 1830 Andrew Jackson passed the Indian Removal Act, which gave lands west of the Mississippi to the Native Americans. The act forced all nations to move out of the eastern states into a **reservation** area. Those who refused to move were rounded up and escorted by the US army. This move is known as the Trail of Tears. It took over a year and by the end of it more than a quarter of the Native Americans had died.

The Cherokees' journey from their lands to the reservations in Oklahoma is known as the Trail of Tears.

The Shawnee chief, Tecumseh.

Through the Plains

An illustration of travellers moving west along the Oregon Trail, with cattle and wagons loaded with all their possessions.

A map of the different trails leading across North America towards California and Oregon.

The battles of the early 19th century did not stop the expansion of the United States.

The reason for this expansion was that land was becoming expensive in the east and more and more people wanted a patch of their own. Traders told stories of the rich and fertile lands on the west coast and soon thousands of families were setting out across the plains heading towards Oregon and California. So many people were travelling west that trails were made, such as the Oregon and California Trails.

The Railway

The trails made in the 1840s cut through the plains and the hunting grounds of the nations living there.

Some of the nations were therefore hostile to the travellers, while others helped them, knowing that the settlers were moving through to another territory. When the railway was built through the plains things began to change. Miners, cattlemen and farmers moved into the area. This led to a period of treaty-making between the nations of the plains and the US government. The Native Americans signed agreements which were instantly broken by the settlers.

The US government believed that the best option for the Native Americans was to put them in reservations, where they could have their own land and become farmers as the settlers were doing. The Native American attitude to this idea was summed up by Big Eagle, a Sioux chief, who said 'The whites were always trying to make the Indians give up their life and live like white men, and the Indians did not know how to do that, and did not want to anyway.'

Reservation Rebellion

When the Native Americans did not stay in their reservations, the army needed little excuse to attack them. In 1864 Colonel John Chivington attacked and killed the Cheyenne chief Black Kettle and his warriors. This action caused the nations of the plains to unite and, in revenge, Chief Red Cloud led the Sioux, Cheyenne and Arapahoe in an ambush against the army and wiped them out.

Dominion of Canada

Further north the government of Great Britain passed the British North America Act in 1867 which gave home rule to the four colonies of Canada. This newly formed country was called the Dominion of Canada and its capital was Ottawa. The new government encouraged settlers to move west on to the lands of the **First Nations**, such as the Cree nation.

Under the leadership of Louis Riel the **Metis** rebelled against the settlers in the Red River Rebellion. Riel presented a list of rights to the government, which included freedom of language and religion, rights to land and a part in the governing of Canada. The Prime Minister agreed to the list. But, as the Canadian Dominion expanded, so did the settlers' territory.

Chief Red Cloud of the Sioux nation.

In 1866 officials from the three provinces of British North America met in London to discuss the conditions of becoming the Dominion of Canada.

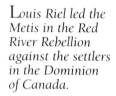

Louis Riel led the Metis in the Red River Rebellion against the settlers in the Dominion of Canada.

The Last Stand

In the 1870s word spread around the United States that gold had been found in the Dakota hills of the Sioux territory. The gold rush began. **Prospectors** surged into the Sioux territory, which the Sioux were determined to keep. In 1876 the government tried to buy the land, but the Sioux refused to accept money. The Sioux chief, Sitting Bull, and other warriors kept leaving their reservation and when they were ordered back they refused to go. The army under General George Custer was called in to force them back. Custer stalked Sitting Bull and his warriors to Little Bighorn where he was defeated by the Sioux warriors. Sitting Bull knew that there would be an outcry, so he escaped to Canada. He returned six months later and surrendered to government troops, who put him back in the reservation.

The Metis

The First Nations in Canada were also trying to keep their old lands and traditions. The Metis, led by Louis 'David' Riel, again tried to resist changes. In 1885 Riel urged all First Nations people to join the Metis' struggle. The resistance was called the Batoche Uprising. It was short-lived. Riel was caught and hanged, while others were imprisoned.

Wounded Knee

The battle at Little Bighorn had made the conflict between the settlers and the Native Americans worse.

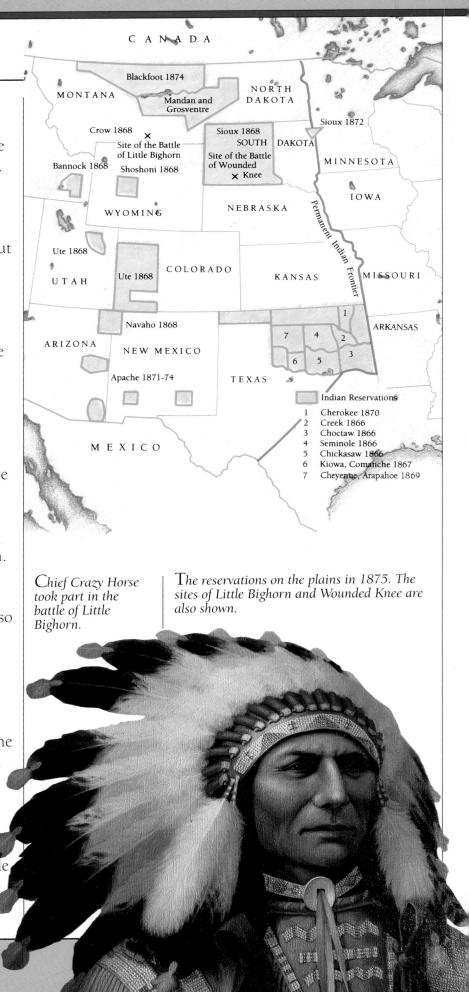

	Indian Reservations
1	Cherokee 1870
2	Creek 1866
3	Choctaw 1866
4	Seminole 1866
5	Chickasaw 1866
6	Kiowa, Comanche 1867
7	Cheyenne, Arapahoe 1869

Chief Crazy Horse took part in the battle of Little Bighorn.

The reservations on the plains in 1875. The sites of Little Bighorn and Wounded Knee are also shown.

In 1890 Sitting Bull was shot for encouraging his people in their desire for freedom. The same year another Sioux chief, Big Foot, decided to take his people to another reservation. On their way they met the US army and had to surrender to them. They were kept overnight in a military camp at Wounded Knee Creek. In the morning the army asked them to give up their guns and other weapons. One young warrior refused and in the struggle a shot was fired. The army massacred all 350 Sioux men, women and children.

This slaughter marks the end of the Native American struggle to keep their lands. The words of a Nez Perce chief, Chief Joseph, sum up what all nations were feeling at this time: 'I am tired of fighting. Our chiefs are killed. The old men are dead. I am tired. My heart is sick and sad. From where the sun now stands I will fight no more forever.'

General George Custer in Montana early in the 1870s with the Native American scouts he used. He and his men were guarding the railway at the time. The man standing at the back by the tent door is thought to be Curly, the only survivor of the battle at Little Bighorn.

Geronimo

In the south-west a treaty signed in 1852 created good relations between the Apaches and the whites. But in 1861 a part-white boy was kidnapped and when Cochise, the chief of the Apaches, offered to help find him, he was himself taken prisoner. He escaped and started attacking the white people of the area. For ten years they were not caught, and, in 1872, a settlement was **negotiated** between Cochise and General Howard. Two years later Cochise died and, while most of the Apaches kept to the settlement, one decided to continue the war. This man was Geronimo.

For five years Geronimo attacked white settlers until he was caught and imprisoned. He escaped but was finally captured again in 1886 and sent to reservations in Alabama and then Oklahoma. He spoke for his nation who had been forced into reservations when he said: 'Our people are decreasing in numbers here, and will continue to decrease unless they are allowed to return to our native land. There is no climate or soil which is equal to that of Arizona. I want to spend my last days there, and be buried among those mountains. If this could be I might die in peace.' He was never able to return to the south-west.

6 The 20th Century

New Treaties

In the late 19th century there was still a great demand from the whites of the United States for land. To break up the large reservations, the General Allotment Act of 1887 was passed. This divided Native American lands into individual portions. The idea was to encourage the Native Americans to farm their own land. This was not the way of any of the nations. They used land for the community, either hunting on it or farming as a group, not as individuals. In 1889 President Harrison decided to open up all the agreed Native American territory to the whites.

In 1890 a group of Comanche men went to Washington to see the United States government. They wanted to discuss territorial rights. In this picture they are all wearing European clothes.

Gaining Recognition

White settlement in the West pushed Native Americans aside onto poor lands and then left them isolated. Native Americans were not even counted as US citizens until 1924. However, they gained a champion in John Collier (1884–1968), who founded the American Indian Defense Association in 1922. As US Commissioner of Indian Affairs (1932–45) he got Congress to pass the Indian Reorganization Act (1934), which recognized the value of tribal cultures in law and the right of tribes to govern themselves. In 1946 the Indian Claims Commission was established which by 1978 would award $800 million compensation to tribes for violations of land rights, guaranteed by treaties. Collier also got government funds to bring them roads and electricity.

A Growing Voice

During World War Two 44,000 Native Americans served in US armed forces. This gained them recognition and respect. Another 40,000 moved away from the reservations to towns and cities where they found new jobs in construction and industry. This enabled native Americans to earn three times as much as before. With more financial control came more freedom. There was, however, still much more to be done.

Native Americans in their reservation at Standing Rock. This photograph was taken around the time of the First World War. The boy in the front is wearing army uniform and waving the American flag.

During the late 19th and early 20th century, people from all over Europe emigrated to North America, which was called the Land of Promise.

Regrowth

The 1950s civil rights movement which moved African-Americans to demand fair treatment, and the 1960s Black Power movement which followed, inspired the foundation of the American Indian Movement. While this drew attention to their grievances, the work of the campaigners was not rewarded immediately. In 1980 more than half of the 1.4 million Native Americans still lived on 270 reservations where a third lived below the poverty line and 40% dropped out of high school.

Changing Attitudes

Public and political attitudes changed as books, Hollywood movies and TV programmes began to present the history of the West from a Native American point of view. Equally important was the success of Native Americans in organizing themselves. In 1965 there were fewer than a dozen Native Americans qualified as lawyers, by 1990 there were over 500. They skilfully used laws designed to protect endangered species or historic properties to fend off further intrusions on tribal lands. The 1973 energy crisis led to the founding of the Council of Energy Resource Tribes to ensure they got best value out of the 15% of the nation's coal and half of all private uranium supplies under their control. Congress has since given legal protection to Native American religions, graves, trails and historic sites. Far from disappearing, as predicted a century ago, Native Americans have at last secured their place in today's United States.

Martin Luther King spoke out for the rights of black Americans. He inspired all oppressed peoples, including Native Americans.

In Canada

Canada was traditionally a refuge for Native Americans fleeing warfare and hunger. The British North America Act (1867) which granted Canada self-government recognized that its native peoples had legal rights but they also came to share the Native Americans' fate of poverty and isolation. The 1927 Indian Act actually forbade them from forming political organizations, speaking in their languages or following their religions. Following the US pattern, they formed the National Indian Council (1961), which grew into the Assembly of First Nations (1982). In 1999 the eastern two-thirds of the former North West Territories, equal in size to Western Europe, became a self-governing homeland for 25,000 Inuit peoples – Nunavut (Our Land). In 2002 the Canadian government introduced a First Nations Governance Act to strengthen tribal powers of self-government.

The Mohawk blocked the roads leading to their sacred burial grounds in the town of Oka, Quebec.

The 100th anniversary of the battle of Wounded Knee. Many of the Sioux and other plains nations gathered to remember their ancestors.

North America	Europe	Other
c.9000 BCE Hunters spread throughout North and South America.	c.6500 BCE Farming begins in Greece and spreads to other areas of Europe.	c.5000 BCE Farming begins in western parts of India.
c.3000 BCE Permanent villages set up by farmers in western North America.	c.3000 BCE Use of copper spreads throughout Europe.	c.2500 BCE The horse is domesticated in Central Asia.
c.1000 CE Vikings land on Newfoundland.	1066 The Normans conquer England.	30 CE The death of Jesus Christ. The spread of Christianity begins.
1492 Columbus lands in the West Indies and Central America.	1492 The first globe is made in Germany by Martin Beheim.	1498 The Portuguese (led by Vasco da Gama) arrive in India.
1534 Jacques Cartier lands at Gaspe and founds New France.	1517 Martin Luther starts the Reformation.	1520 Suleiman I becomes Sultan of the Ottoman Empire.
1560 Formation of the Iroquois League of First Nations.	1532 John Calvin starts the Protestant movement in France.	1530 The European slave trade begins across the Atlantic Ocean.
1603 Samuel de Champlain sails down the St Lawrence River.	1569 Gerardus Mercator publishes his first world map.	1577 Francis Drake leaves England to search for Terra Australis.
1626 The Dutch buy Manhattan Island for £15 from the Manhattas nation.	1618 The Thirty Years War of religion starts.	1644 The Manchu Dynasty in China.
1681 Penn signs a treaty with Native Americans over Pennsylvania.	1667 The French begin to expand under Louis XIV.	1680 The Rozvi Empire in Zimbabwe.
1732 Creek nation welcomes Georgia settlers, led by James Oglethorpe.	1707 England and Scotland unite.	c.1700s European exploration of Africa.
1763 Royal proclamation recognizes Native American rights to land.	1756 The Seven Years War begins.	1750 The Asante kingdom is at its most powerful in west Africa.
1775-1783 Thirteen colonies revolt against British government and finally gain the Declaration of Independence.	c.1760 The Age of Enlightenment.	1772-75 James Cook circumnavigates. Antarctica.
1789 George Washington becomes the first President of the United States.	1789 The French Revolution begins.	1775 War starts in India between the British and the Marathas.
1861 The American Civil War begins.	1807 The slave trade is abolished. in Britain.	1817-22 Chile, Mexico, Venezuela, Brazil, Colombia and Ecuador gain independence.
1876 Sitting Bull and the Sioux defeat General Custer at Little Big Horn.	1884-85 The West African conference is held in Berlin (Germany).	1857 The Indian Mutiny.
1890 US cavalry kill 350 Sioux people at Wounded Knee.	1904 Queen Victoria dies.	1905 The start of the Russian Revolution.
1917 The USA enters the First World War.	1914-18 The First World War.	1923 Turkey is made a republic.
1941 The US enters the Second World War.	1939-45 The Second World War.	1947 India gains independence.
1952-58 US Congress develops Termination Resolution, which eliminates Native American reservations.	1961 The Berlin Wall is built in Germany.	1985 Mikhail Gorbachev becomes leader of the Soviet Union.
1973 Militant Native Americans occupy Wounded Knee.	1972 The European Community gains more members.	1989 Boris Yeltsin becomes leader of Russia.
1990 Native American Graves Protection and Repatriation Act. 2002 Canadian First Nations Governance Act.	1992 Yugoslavia breaks up.	1993 Nelson Mandela is voted President of South Africa.

Glossary

A

Algonquian: the base language spoken by many First Nations from the north-eastern woodlands to the plains.

C

chart: to draw up maps which help sailors and travellers to find their way.

clan: a group of people linked by birth and marriage.

colonies: groups of people who settle in a land far from their homeland, but keep ties with it.

commission: a task which is authorized by the Crown or a government.

conquistador: an adventurer or conqueror, particularly someone from Spain in the 16th century.

D

domesticate: to tame and keep wild animals on farms or in households.

draft: to force people to join the army, navy or air force.

E

Equator: the imaginary line around the middle of the world dividing it into two equal halves.

evolve: to develop gradually.

F

fertile: land which produces a good crop because its soil is moist and full of minerals for the plants to feed on.

First Nations: a modern name which many Native Americans (especially in Canada) use to describe themselves because their ancestors were the first people to live in North America.

G

glacier: a huge, slow-moving mass of ice.

governor: a person appointed to rule an area such as a **colony** or province.

H

habitable: an area of land in which animals, plants and people can easily live.

I

immigrants: people who move to a country which is not their homeland in order to settle there.

Iroquois: the base language of nations such as the Cherokee, Mohawk, Oneida, Cayuga, Seneca, Onondaga and Huron.

K

katchina: the spirits worshipped by the Native Americans of the south-west. They were thought to influence birth, death and rebirth.

M

mastodons: large elephant-like animals which are now extinct.

Metis: children born of a mixed marriage. One parent is European and the other is Native American. The Metis **nation** was formed in the 19th century.

missionaries: people who travel to other lands to spread a religious faith.

N

nations: the term used to describe groups of Native Americans, who lived and travelled together as a unit.

negotiate: to talk and discuss possibilities in order to reach an agreement.

nomadic: a word used to describe people who constantly move from place to place in search of good land or food.

P

pagan gods: gods worshipped in religions that are not Christian, Muslim or Jewish.

passive solar heating: a way of heating homes using the sun's rays. The walls of the houses are warmed up during the day and release heat into the houses when the sun goes down.

peninsula: a narrow strip of land sticking out into the sea from the mainland.

persimmon: an orange fruit which grows on trees.

prospectors: people who search and explore different regions for particular substances, such as gold or oil.

Q

Quaker: a member of the Society of Friends, a Christian sect founded by George Fox in 1650. The central belief is the idea of Inner Light.

R

reservation: an area of land set aside by various authorities for Native Americans to live on and work as their own.

ritual: the established way of performing a religious ceremony.

S

social services: welfare provided by the government for a community, such as child-minding, schools and rubbish collecting.

squash: an edible, marrow-like plant with a thick skin and soft flesh.

stability: a steadiness and feeling of security.

staple foods: the main foods that people eat, such as potatoes or corn.

T

tobacco: a plant found in North America. The dried leaves are smoked or chewed.

treaty: an agreement made between governments from different countries to bring about peace or better relations.

tundra: a treeless plain in Arctic regions.

Index

Numbers in **bold** indicate
an illustration. Words in
bold are in the glossary
on page 47.

This edition published in 2003 by
Belitha Press
A member of Chrysalis Books plc
64 Brewery Road, London N7 9NT

Copyright © in this format Belitha Press
Illustrations copyright © Robina Green
Text copyright © Bill Asikinack and Kate Scarborough

ISBN 1 84138 646 4

Typeset by Chambers Wallace, London

Printed in Hong Kong

British Library Cataloguing in Publication Data for this book
is available from the British Library.

Editor: Kate Scarborough
Designer: Simon Borrough
Picture researcher: Juliet Duff
Consultant: Trudy Hamner
Map annotation: Hardlines
Illustration on page 22: Deborah Kindred

Photographic credits

Bridgeman Art Library 3, 14 National Museum of American
Art, Smithsonian, Permlet Art Resource, 10 Royal Ontario
Museum, Toronto, 15 right Christie's, London, 26 bottom
Sheffield City Art Galleries, 27 top Private Collection, 32
bottom National Gallery of Canada, Ontario, 35 bottom
Chateau de Versailles, France/Lauros-Giraudon; ET Archive
21 top Bibliotheque Nationale, Paris, 23 New York Public
Library, 24 bottom British Museum, 32 top NT Quebec
House, Kent; Werner Forman Archive 9 bottom Museum of
Mankind, London, 11 left Private collection, New York, 12
top Museum of the American Indian, Heye Foundation, New
York, 16 top, 16 bottom Maxwell Museum of Anthropology,
Albuquerque, NM, USA, 16-17, 17 Schindler Collection,
New York, 19 top left, 19 top right Portland Art Museum,
Oregon, USA, 19 centre Provincial Museum, Victoria, British
Columbia; Michael Holford: 8; Magnum Photos title page
David Alan Harvey, 12 bottom Fred Mayer, 44 Bob
Henriques; Mansell Collection 11 right, 25 centre left, 34
bottom; Mirror Syndication 15 left, 18 left Smithsonian
Institute, 29 top National Gallery of Art, Washington Paul
Mellon Collection, 30 bottom Aldus, 31 BPCC/Aldus, 35 top
United State Information Service; Peter Newark's Historical
Pictures 6 bottom, 7 bottom, 13 both, 21 bottom, 22 top,
25 top, 26 top, 27 bottom, 28 both, 30 top, 34 top, 36 top,
37 bottom, 38 top, 39 top and centre, 40 bottom, 43
bottom; NHPA 18 right; Range Pictures 9 top, 25 centre
right, 37 top, 39 bottom, 41 both, 42, 43 top; Frank
Spooner Pictures 45 both; Zefa 2, 6 top.

Front cover: (background) Tony Stone Images;
(foreground) Zefa
Back cover: Tony Stone Images.